Reimagining the Spiritual Disciplines for a Di[illegible]e

Sara Schumacher

Tutor and Lecturer in Theology and the Arts

GROVE BOOKS LIMITED
RIDLEY HALL RD CAMBRIDGE CB3 9HU

Contents

Acknowledgments

The existence of this manuscript is indebted to many: to my students at St Mellitus who have sharpened my thinking with their questions and insights; to Philip Seddon for his patient direction and insightful comments throughout the writing and editing process; to Thomas Brauer for his beautiful photography; to the Rev'd Dr Donna Lazenby, a constant encourager and brilliant dialogue partner as the ideas have developed over the past few years; and to my Connect Group as we have journeyed together in our practice of the disciplines. I am grateful for you all.

First Impression May 2020
ISSN 0262-799X
ISBN 978 1 78827 122 6

Preface

1

This booklet started out as a lecture I gave at a summer conference in 2016.[1] I was speaking on a seminar stream titled 'The Renewal of your Mind,' and, at the time, I was interested in the interplay between embodiment and the digital, specifically how technology was changing the physicality of our brains by forming new neural pathways.[2] In my reading of wider literature, I had started to notice that scholars in fields such as sociology and psychology were, with consistency, observing that engaging in certain practices was key to retaining our humanity in a digital age. While secular in orientation, I also noticed that, while not intending to, these scholars were advocating for a recovery of what Christians have known as the classical spiritual disciplines. While scholars could give no reason why they were efficacious apart from observation, I found myself asking if we, as the church, had anything to learn from their (re)discovery. By bringing these scholars into conversation with classic authors such as Richard Foster, in the original lecture I suggested how we, as Christians, could use these insights to recover as well as reimagine our practice of the spiritual disciplines in a digital age. I ended by posing this question: 'Might a serious reclaiming of the disciplines, stepping into the pattern of life that forms us into Christ's image, be a way that our minds are renewed not only spiritually but also physically, possibly subverting the vulnerabilities that technology has exposed us to?'

Might reclaiming the disciplines be a way that our minds are renewed?

The response to this lecture was surprising. It demonstrably resonated deeply with those in the room and resulted in multiple invitations to deliver the content in other contexts, ultimately culminating in this Grove booklet. However, two things have changed since then that warrant this preface. In 2016 there were very few voices in this discussion, and church use of digital technology was usually justified by pragmatism with little critical or theological engagement as to its impact.[3] However, nearly four years on, Christian thinking on this has exploded with books being published that make similar claims to my own book.[4] This indicates that the need is real, and that the disciplines have something significant to offer contemporary, digital life. The second change has been in me. Invitations to deliver this content have meant that I have read, taught and meditated a lot on what it means to practise faithfulness in a digital age. In 2016, my spiritual practices were present but sporadic. There was no rhythm in my life to the degree I was advocating. But the Spirit would not let me be, sending me back again and again to the truth of what it means to follow Jesus faithfully while fully inhabiting the world we are in. In this booklet, I have decided to share some of how my own life has changed as I have sought to live out the content. My prayer for you is that as you practise faithfulness you will know the transforming work of the Spirit and the freedom found in becoming like Christ.

Introducing the Digital Age

2

'Culture is most powerful...when it is perceived as self-evident.'[5] While the sociologist James Davison Hunter is not speaking specifically about the digital age, his observation is a helpful starting point for introducing the digital age and exploring its power in our lives. What Hunter means is that when culture becomes self-evident, or 'the way things are,' we no longer ask the question *why* because it just simply is. Because we no longer ask *why,* we no longer ask *if* things should be the way they are. Thus we become blind to culture's impact, for it is simply the water we swim in. For the twenty-first century, this water is the revolution and impact of the, now self-evident, digital age.

Beginning in the mid-twentieth century and taking a particular turn with the rise of social media and handheld digital devices in the early part of the twenty-first, the advent of the digital age is not simply the addition of new tools for communication. Instead, we now inhabit a new space for human living. At the surface, the digital age has changed the way we communicate, bank, travel, play and read, and will continue to do so, consigning many analogue ways of life to the past. As we use these tools, how we experience and perceive the world is also changing.[6] Categories of time and space, once perceived as bound, are being renegotiated. For example, for some, geography no longer determines community, so relationships no longer require the physical embodiment or proximity that they once did. Further, when the opportunity came to connect with those separated by time and distance, 2.7 billion of us have jumped at the chance to create a Facebook profile and rekindle those friendships. Back then (in 2007), most of us were not thinking about privacy or what this reconnection would do to our concept of what it means to be a friend. Instead, we were captivated by the transcendence of the limitations that this new technology was enabling for the first time.

The advent of the digital age is not simply the addition of new tools for communication

However, the temperature of the water has changed. We are now starting to take notice of the impact of the digital age on us, as humans. While technology creates significant opportunity to reinforce relationships, we are, at the same time, in danger of isolation. We can be alone together, existing in each other's embodied presence but not present in mind or attention.[7] Further, the information silos created by the algorithms of social media mean that our own political, religious and / or cultural perspectives are only reinforced rather than challenged, preventing us from engaging with real difference in a meaningful and transformative way. Finally, the automation of digital technology in the workplace has led to lone working while also displacing a significant proportion of people from the workplace altogether. While we have gained, we have also lost, and we are now trying to understand how much those losses matter. As we seek to figure out how to live in this new digital reality, deep questions that have lain dormant because answers were believed to be secure, have started to bubble up to the surface. What does it mean to love my global neighbour that I can now 'see'? Can a machine love me? If so, what is love? Can machines help us to transcend the limitations of our humanity? Should they? Does embodiment matter? More fundamentally, we are asking, what does it mean to be human? What does it mean to live well as a human in a digital age? This final question is the focus of this booklet.

For the Christian, what it means to live well as a human is not a new pursuit. A life well lived is a life lived in faithful obedience to Christ, and the practices of Christian spirituality have been central to this aim. However, the latter part—in a digital age—is what is new, and it is sociologists and social psychologists who have led the way in observing how digital technology impacts how we relate to one another, to ourselves, and to the world around us. From this research, a consistent message is emerging: *if we do not control technology, it will control us.* While technology can be a gift, it is not neutral, and left to its own ends, it will dominate us. This has been given specific attention by a range of recent publications: Cal Newport, Associate Professor of Computer Science at Georgetown University, advocates a lifestyle marked by *digital minimalism* in order to increase productivity and rediscover meaning in our 'analogue life';[8] Sherry Turkle, Professor of the Social Studies of Science and Technology at Massachusetts Institute of Technology, insists that *reclaiming conversation* is the means to recover that which is essential to being human, specifically restoring the capacity for empathy between embodied persons;[9] Susan Pinker, a clinical psychologist and author, reminds us of the importance of the village, of deep and local community, as an antidote to loneliness in a digital age;[10] and Adam Alter, Associate Professor of Marketing at New York University, shows how all of us can become addicted under the right conditions and how we are particularly vulnerable to the irresistibility designed into technology.[11]

If we do not control technology, it will control us

While the range of voices is wide, none are concluding that the solution is a return to a pre-digital age, a nostalgic fantasy that causes us to overlook all that the digital age has made possible. Instead, each, in their own way, is advocating a type of discipline. To live well as humans in a digital age, we must put in place practices or habits that control our use of digital technology so that, as noted earlier, it does not control us. Newport suggests we start with a 30-day digital fast to strip away the digital build-up that clouds our ability to remember what is meaningful. He also argues that we must reintroduce the discipline of solitude into our daily lives.[12] Turkle also identifies solitude as key to retaining our humanity as individuals and fostering healthy, empathetic community.[13] Alter, to combat the addictive capacity in all of us, advocates for habits and 'behavioural architecture' that allows us to live well with technology without being seduced into overuse.[14] Put another way, solitude, simplicity of life and rest from technology are key to a life well lived. While not articulated as such, if we read this work with a Christian imagination, we find traces of the classical spiritual disciplines.

While there is a limit to how far we can use these conclusions because they are embedded in the assumptions of their respective fields, nonetheless, I want to suggest that they are important conversation partners for Christians seeking to live a faithful, disciplined life. This is because they provide a different lens through which to recover and reimagine our own spiritual practice in a digital age. Even further, Christian theology offers something back to these writers, specifically an explanation for why these disciplines lead to human flourishing. They are not simply given or evolutionary; instead, they evidence a God-given order in creation.

These disciplines evidence a God-given order in creation

This booklet is divided into two parts. I begin by considering what it means to live well and the role of the spiritual disciplines to this end. From here, I will discuss three classical spiritual disciplines—solitude, simplicity and Sabbath—and use the authors above to recover and reimagine our Christian practice for a digital age. For each, I will provide a short description of how Christian spirituality has understood what this discipline is, bring that into conversation with contemporary secular writing, and draw out some principles for practice.

3 Living Well and Discipline

The desire to live well is a growing concern within contemporary culture, articulated in a variety of ways, such as 'human flourishing,' 'the common good' or the 'good life.' The desire has been made acute by the implications of the changes (and the rate of change) brought on by digital technology. For example, while inequality has always existed, digital technology has now made that visible. Further, social media has given platforms to voices that institutions would, in the past, have silenced. The shift from analogue to digital is happening so quickly that, for many, it feels like the ground is shifting beneath their feet, with chaos and uncertainty characterizing this cultural moment. In light of this, it is not surprising that questions of living well are a concern, with attainment of the good life a goal.

Relevant to the aims of this booklet, what we tend to characterize as the good life has always been dependent on discipline of some sort. A healthy body does not happen without discipline in eating, exercise and sleep. Education does not happen without disciplining one's mind in the activity of study, reading, writing and experimenting. Natural gifts are not developed without learning foundational skills and the discipline of subsequent practice. Friendship does not happen without learning how to converse, empathize and discipline our own selfish compulsions. Discipline is a part of what it means for us to be human and live in this world. To be disciplined is something we aspire to as humans, as evidenced by the types of resolutions we tend to make at the start of each year.

Discipline has always been central to the life of the church

The importance of discipline has always been central to the life of the church. Seen as early as Acts 2.42–47, the disciplined Christian life has been a mark of spiritual maturity, and the spiritual disciplines have been key to this end. While some might want to argue that the disciplines lead to legalism and are contrary to the spontaneous and extemporaneous life of the Spirit, in reality, the purpose of the spiritual disciplines, as Richard Foster puts it, is 'liberation from the stifling slavery to self-interest and fear.'[15] They are the 'door to liberation' rather than its hindrance.[16] As 'a means of receiving [God's] grace,' these Christian habits 'allow us to place ourselves before God so that he can transform us.'[17] While never an end in themselves—a vital distinction from the disciplines of secular society—Christian practices put us in a place to be transformed by the Spirit into the image of the Son. As we carve patterns into our lives in line with how God designed us to live, we demonstrate our desire to know God and 'keep company with Jesus.'[18]

Further, we practise the disciplines because God calls us to faithfulness and obedience. These practices are known by their outward manifestations, such as: prayer, fasting, study, worship, solitude and simplicity. However, an outward manifestation without an inward orientation towards God does collapse into legalism.[19] Thus, cultivating outward practice must be matched by interrogating what is happening in our heart, soul, mind and spirit, inviting the Spirit to illuminate the areas in our life that are 'de-formed' and submitting to his reformation. The genesis of our practice is a longing after God and a longing for deeper intimacy with our creator, the one who authors the true good life. It is as we come to know our creator that we are able to answer the existential questions on the lips of contemporary society. From this place of intimacy, we recover our creatureliness.

Recovering our Creatureliness

Christians live in a paradox: while fully present in and to the world, we are, at the same time, not of the world.[20] We are called to be in the world and are gifted by God to be cultivators of the creation that he has made (Gen 1.27). We live as embodied beings, able to take in through our senses all the beauty that is around us. Fully in the world, we are free to use our human creativity and take what is in front of us to make it into something else. However, while this creativity is gift, we also live in the world where, because of the fall, sin has permeated everything. While we are created for God, our fallenness curves us in on ourselves and displaces God as the one at the centre of our lives. Thus, our creativity is used for selfish gain rather than service to the other.

Being conformed into the image of Christ is a struggle

It is from this paradox that the spiritual disciplines emerge. While sin means separation, because of the grace of the Father in the work of Christ and through the power of the Holy Spirit, the way is made back to relationship with God. While our way back to the Father is pure gift, being conformed into the image of Christ is a struggle. We do what we do not want to do and do not do what we do want to do, words penned by Paul that so accurately describe our human reality (Rom 7.19). Thus, while saved by grace, Christians are in a battle of formation: whose image are we being formed into? Who are we becoming like?

When Adam and Eve asserted their independence over God, displacing him as the one who is Lord over all (Genesis 3), so entered our human struggle to understand who we truly are. When God is displaced as creator, we forget that we are creatures. When this happens, we start to believe that *we* are creator, and follow Adam and Eve down the path of pseudo-godlikeness.[21] However, rather than the unlimited freedom that we crave and are told to pursue and preserve in Western culture, we find ourselves in bondage to a distorted view of who we are. Anxiety, fear, dis-ease and unrest sink in as we face the consequences of making ourselves the centre of the universe, a place we cannot sustain and are not created to inhabit.

This is why the spiritual disciplines are so important. As we intentionally practise the way of the Spirit, we experience the freedom that comes with discipline. When we live in a way marked by the story of the gospel, the cultural narrative of unlimited freedom loses its power and allure. As our bodies practise faith, our minds learn that God is the creator upon whom we are wholly dependent for life itself (1 Cor 8.6). Rather than life being entirely what we make of it, we learn that we are finite but loved, sustained in all things by our loving Father. From here, our frame of reference shifts, making us able to see that all is gift. Rather than striving or hustling or hurrying, as God's creatures we can let go and be free to participate in the story that God has written into creation.[22] About this, Stanley Hauerwas says, 'To be human is to learn that we don't get to make up our lives because we're creatures. Christians are people who recognize that we have a Father whom we can thank for our existence. Christian discipleship is about learning to receive our life as gift without regret.'[23] To be free from regret is only possible when we live our embodied lives in a way that reinforces the truth that we are not God. To this end, the spiritual disciplines provide the 'trellis' upon which we can build our faithful practice.[24]

Freedom comes with discipline

With this as the foundation, we turn to consider three of the classical spiritual disciplines that emerge in various forms in the work of those writing about the good life in the digital age, specifically the practices of solitude, simplicity and Sabbath.

Reimagining the Practice of the Spiritual Disciplines: Solitude

4

For those writing about the digital age, solitude is under particular threat in our time. Newport goes so far as to say that we live in a time of 'solitude deprivation,' describing it as '[a] state in which you spend close to zero time alone with your own thoughts and free from input from other minds.'[25] He continues, 'We need solitude to thrive as human beings, and in recent years, without even realizing it, we've been systematically reducing this crucial ingredient from our lives.'[26] Turkle is also concerned for the loss of solitude, specifically its effect on how we relate to each other. For her, '[t]he capacity for solitude makes relationships with others more authentic. Because you know who you are, you can see others for who they are, not for who you need them to be.'[27] Without a secure sense of the self that is generated in the practice of being alone, 'we turn to other people to support our sense of self.'[28] While digital technology promises human connection, because it erodes our capacity for solitude, the quality of our relationships with others is diminished. For all these reasons and more, if digital technology is creating a solitude deprivation, as Christians, we should be equally concerned, for we are not immune.

In Christian spirituality, solitude is a container discipline, meaning it makes the practice of the other disciplines possible. If we can cultivate a practice of solitude, we create the scaffolding for other disciplines. We practise solitude by 'scheduling enough uninterrupted time in a distraction-free environment;'[29] however, rather than being 'alone with our thoughts,' which is one of Newport's aims,[30] we 'experience isolation and are alone with God.'[31] In the life of Christ, we see the gospels record time and again his practice of seeking solitude: when he began his ministry (Matt 4.1–11); before choosing his apostles (Luke 6.12); after receiving news of John the Baptist's death (Matt 14.13); and after times of significant ministry (Matt 14.23; Mark 6.31). Jesus sought time alone with the Father, often in the midst of busyness, and, we are invited to do the same. While solitude might involve a 'lonely place,' it is 'more a state of mind and heart.'[32] As we are alone with God, solitude helps us to cultivate an inward attentiveness to the activity of God in our lives and in the world. In this place, we are laid bare before our creator, aware of our vulnerability but, crucially, safe. Solitude puts us in the place to be transformed by the Spirit into our true identity as a child of God.

Solitude helps us cultivate attentiveness to the activity of God in our lives

From this place of intimacy, we learn something important about ourselves: 'If we possess inward solitude we do not fear being alone, for we know that we are not alone.'[33] In a world where loneliness has now been declared an epidemic, to advocate solitude can feel unkind. However, Newport and others are right to be concerned about solitude deprivation for, according to Christian spirituality, solitude is the antidote to loneliness rather than its synonym. Richard Foster describes the difference like this: 'Loneliness is inner emptiness. Solitude is inner fulfilment.'[34] Solitude is inner fulfilment not because we are alone with our own thoughts but because we are alone with the God of the universe who is sustaining all things (Col 1.17), meaning we are never truly alone. Solitude is something we practise but it is also an invitation to be present, in this moment, before our God. To deprive ourselves of solitude separates us from ourselves (Newport), others (Turkle) and God (Foster). Technology tells us being alone is a problem it can solve by continuous connection.[35] The cruel twist is this: 'If we are unable to be alone, we will be more lonely.'[36] Thus, reimagining the practice of solitude in light of the digital age we are in is vital.

Solitude is an invitation to be present, in this moment, before our God

The challenges of practising and cultivating solitude are not new for the Christian. While finding physical space for solitude can be difficult, Richard Foster suggests that 'the first thing we can do is to take advantage of the "little solitudes" that fill our day...these tiny snatches of time are often lost to us...they can and should be redeemed. They are times for inner quiet, for reorientating our lives like a compass needle. They are little moments that help us to be genuinely present where we are.'[37] Newport further expands on where our 'tiny snatches of time' are being lost: to the 'quick glance' at our portable digital devices.[38] This move from occasional to continuous disruption means that, on average, we are spending a quarter of our time on our phones, checking for new notifications an average of thirty-nine times a day.[39] For Newport, to regain control over our time, we have to become aware of the power of our digital devices. To this end, he suggests that we embark on a 'digital declutter' in order to remember and realign ourselves with the things, practices and people that bring value to our life. The declutter is, in Christian terms, a fast from our engagement with digital devices and applications for thirty days. The fast is necessary because our digital use layers up over time. The speed at which technology develops, changes and imposes itself on us becomes like a thick film that accumulates on a window, making it hard to see through to what we really love and desire. Taking a break exposes where it has taken control.[40] We need to heed Newport's suggestion to declutter in order to regain space and time for solitude, so that we can listen to God and reconnect with each other and ourselves. It is from this place that we will notice the 'little solitudes' that Foster advocates we recover.

Solitude in Practice: Reclaiming My Commute

With the contents of this booklet fresh in my mind, I started to discern an uncomfortable prompting of the Spirit in my own spiritual practice of solitude. I am no longer a big user of social media and have always been mostly disciplined when using my phone. However, I have a daily commute to and from work and, for as long as I have had my smartphone, this commute has always commenced with the following ritual: putting in my headphones and choosing the podcast or album that will be the soundtrack for my journey. While this is not a bad thing, as Lent approached, I knew that God was asking me to do the following: rather than fill your ears with the voices of others, *leave your headphones at home* in order to cultivate the silence needed for solitude.

So, on Ash Wednesday, with a sense of expectancy and dread in equal measure, I started my walk to and from work with my ears open to the world. Truthfully, the first couple of days were liberating. The novelty of the practice brought energy and enthusiasm. But then, the tiny snatches of time and solitude became…boring. My walk was more tedious than I realized, and time seemed to stretch. Staying with my thoughts was uncomfortable as my mind raced through all that I needed to do, skimming the surface of the day ahead or just gone. Most often, I found myself impatient and irritated, with the people around me as well as myself.

But, as the days went on and I persisted, something started to happen. As the thoughts in my mind started to unknot and unravel, I found myself forced to face what was below the surface: fears, anxieties, questions, problems, hopes, dreams and desires. Facing the truth of myself with no option of escape drove me to prayer for that which needed transformation in my life. Silence allowed for the solitude that attuned me to areas of repentance, while the recovered time and space helped me to see the world, myself and others more clearly. Further, since I was no longer being sucked into the interior world of my headphones, I became more attentive to what was right in front of me. As attention was cultivated, I started to feel compassion and empathy for the world I was now fully present to, leading me to prayer for my neighbour rather than just myself. However, what was most surprising was how solitude restored my creativity. What I had not realized was that in distracting myself from the boredom, I had also dulled my ability to push into the deeper places where creativity and innovation lie, diminishing this aspect of my God-given humanity. The simple act of leaving my headphones at home transformed a

Solitude restored my creativity

daily walk of twenty minutes into time and space for creativity, restoration, prayer, and attentiveness to the creator of the universe.

In a world where time is increasingly our most precious commodity and creating space for solitude is necessary for the fullest expression of our humanity, proactively redeeming the tiny snatches of time that are already there but that we have given over to our digital devices must become an expression in our practise of solitude. We must interrogate our practice, discerning with the Spirit how our use of technology should come under his control. With solitude as a container, we can then move to a practice of simplicity.[41]

Questions for Reflection

- What would a 'Digital Declutter' look like in your life? What does decluttering reveal about what you truly value and about what gives you life?
- Where can you, as Foster suggests, 'take advantage of the "little solitudes" that fill [y]our day'? How can you cultivate silence so that you can listen to the voice of God?
- As you cultivate solitude, what other disciplines can now be brought into your Christian practice?
- How can the discipline of solitude be practised corporately? As we seek to be attentive to Christ in our worship, how can these same principles be applied to gathered church life?

Reimagining the Practice of the Spiritual Disciplines: Simplicity 5

In our contemporary age, simplicity is *en vogue*. As a case in point, the start of 2019 welcomed the Netflix phenomenon, *Tidying Up with Marie Kondo*, a show based on Kondo's bestselling book, *The Life-Changing Magic of Tidying Up*, first published in English in 2014.[42] As we watched in droves, Kondo helped people to bring simplicity to their material lives, getting rid of those possessions that did not spark joy. Through the series, it was not only homes that were decluttered. As participants were released from the burden of possessions, lives were changed: widows were able to grieve, hospitality to parents was able to be extended and time with children was restored. For a society that is characterized as secular, *Tidying Up* was remarkably spiritual. Kondo began each session by acknowledging the presence in the home, sitting on the floor in order to be attuned to the spirit in the place and thanking the house for all that it had done so far for the family. In the tidying-up process, Kondo encouraged participants to thank each item for its service before getting rid of it. The object was acknowledged to be more than an object. It was also a bearer of memory and humanity.

We are seeking simplicity in the turbulence of the times we are in

It makes sense that we are seeking simplicity in the turbulence and uncertainty of the times we are in. While the rise of digital technology has caused us to ask new questions about what it means to be human, world events and globalization have disrupted the *status quo*, challenging the values that the Western world has built its institutions upon. Add to this the ecological crisis and it is no wonder that people feel disorientated. We are desperately seeking simplicity: we want to bring order to the chaos, as the popularity of *Tidying Up* shows. While the particular way we are seeking simplicity might be unique to this moment, what is not unique is the human desire and struggle for simplicity. When we displaced God as the centre of our lives and put ourselves there instead, we invited the kind of complexity that brings bondage rather than freedom (Genesis 3). Christian spirituality undoes this complexity. Simplicity is about learning to let go, 'loosening inordinate attachment to owning and having,' bringing 'freedom and with it generosity' as we learn to trust fully in the provision of God.[43]

To seek a life marked by simplicity requires that we ask ourselves this question: what are we paying attention to? The reason this is important is twofold. One, we are formed by what we give our attention to, for it indicates to us what we truly value.[44] This is why we are commanded to seek first God's kingdom: this is the treasure hidden in a field and the pearl of great value, worth selling all we own in order to obtain (Matt 13.44–45). Thinking about this in light of our digital age, one of the challenges we face is our exposure to lives that are presented to us as seemingly better than our own. As we pay attention to the carefully curated lives of celebrities (or friends), our vision of the good life is slowly formed into that image and away from God's kingdom. Subsequently, what we desire starts to align behind this deformed vision. This relates to the second reason why simplicity is important: what we give our attention to becomes that which we believe our goal to be.[45] When the unattainable becomes our goal, we find ourselves bound to the impossible. The negative impact on mental health, particularly the impact of constant comparison via social media on our sense of self-worth, is now common knowledge.

What we give our attention to becomes that which we believe our goal to be

Christian simplicity teaches us that becoming like Christ and seeking his kingdom, with confidence that it will be fully established in the age to come, is the goal. Through the work of Christ, we have been adopted into God's family, where we are forgiven, accepted, loved, chosen and valued. This is the identity, the centre, around which our lives are designed to be orientated. While our digital devices draw our attention to that which is fleeting, the discipline of simplicity draws us back to our true centre, giving us the resources to live the life that God intends. As we saw with solitude, when the inward reality that we are not God takes root, we are able to let go outwardly. Simplicity is marked by trusting, as Jesus promised, that from this place of simple focus on seeking his kingdom, we are free from anxiety for 'all these things will be added as well' (Matt 6.33). To practise the discipline of simplicity is to practise faithfulness towards Christlikeness, trusting that the rest will follow. Practising the Christian discipline of simplicity today is not simply about how we use our digital devices, although it includes that. Simplicity includes how we live in this world that is now made possible through the technology of our age. It is learning to see how it is forming and shaping who we think we are. However, we must do this aware of how technology is designed to operate in our lives, which is our next point of consideration.

Technology and Addiction

For those writing about how to live well in a digital age, the addictive nature of digital technology is a growing area of concern for scholars such as Adam Alter. He argues that in the past, we have tended to think that developing addictions was limited to those with addictive personalities. However, neuroscience has shown that all of us are capable of becoming addicted under the right conditions, such as when we are rewarded with strong social connection or receive unpredictable positive feedback. As any user knows, these are some of the conditions embedded in the design of digital technology and its applications, which leads Alter to conclude that addiction lies latent in technology's foundations.[46] This is further exacerbated by the revelation that many designers of technology do not let their own children use it for fear of them becoming addicted.[47] To understand the nature of the addiction we face, let us return to the two conditions that make addiction more likely: social connection and unpredictable, positive feedback.

Made in God's image, we are created to love God and love one another (Gen 1.26; Matt 22.37–40). While neuroscience has discovered that 'humans are wired to be social,' this is something that Christianity has always known.[48] This is why loneliness and isolation are so destructive, both to our mental and physical health.[49] Thus, when a social network comes along and promises us relationship and connection, it is not surprising that we, as social animals, jump to take part. While the relational possibility attracts us, the unpredictable, positive feedback keeps us there. For Newport, the advent of a 'Like' button, beginning with Facebook and now ubiquitous across most platforms, is what shifted social media 'from a fun amusement that people occasionally checked, to a digital slot machine that began to dominate its users' time and attention.'[50] When we post, we have no control over how our friends/followers will respond, thus setting the conditions for the unpredictable positive feedback that is the addiction. We keep returning to our account to see if there are more likes, retweets, shares or comments, which can change by the minute, requiring that we compulsively return 'just to check.' When the number goes up, a shot of dopamine fills our body and we feel the reward of the feedback.[51] It is no wonder that studies show that nearly 40% of us suffer from a form of internet-based addiction.[52]

To practise simplicity in a digital age requires constant interrogation of our use of technology

Within Christian spirituality, simplicity is the antidote to addiction. As we orientate our lives to seek first God's kingdom, acknowledging he is the creator and we are his beloved creatures who are free to receive our lives as gift from God, we are able to see clearly *what* has become an addiction. Crucially, we have somewhere to go with this realization, for we can 'decide to open this corner of (our lives) to the forgiving grace and healing power of God.'[53] Because we live in a time where the technology that structures our society means we cannot escape from its presence, to practise simplicity in a digital age requires constant, honest interrogation of our use of technology. This is particularly important while technology is designed for addiction. Until this changes, we have to be wise, resisting the deception that willpower alone will suffice. This means that we have to put in place outward lifestyle changes to support and reinforce the inward reality. For example, a now common suggestion is to buy an alarm clock and charge your phone in a different part of the house. The reason: 'Whatever's nearby will have a bigger impact on your mental life than whatever is farther away.'[54] If your phone is by your head when you sleep, every morning and evening will require active resistance to the temptation to engage. And research indicates we are not doing well in our resistance: 'Ninety-five per cent of adults use an electronic device that emits light in the hour before bed, and more than half check their emails overnight. Sixty per cent of adults aged between eighteen and sixty-four keep their phones next to them when they sleep, which might explain why fifty per cent of adults claim they don't sleep well because they're always connected to technology.'[55]

For the Christian, it is not only sleep quality that is impacted. If we look at Scripture, the times of 'when you lie down and when you get up' are sacred (Deut 6.7).[56] As seen in many of the psalms, morning and evening are times set apart for God, marked by meditation, prayer and solitude.[57] If the research is correct, our phones are not only taking our sleep but are also crowding out our time with God. As we have seen, when we forget who God is, we forget who we are. Rather than seeking first the kingdom of God, single-mindedly focused on our true identity in Christ, the danger is we become de-formed by our false desires. Rather than giving over the start and end of your day to your phone notifications, the discipline of simplicity creates space for solitude and thus for the other disciplines, such as prayer, worship and meditation. Guard those precious moments with all your heart and with eyes open to the 'undisciplined compulsions' that need to be brought under the control of the Spirit.[58]

Simplicity in Practice: Who am I Becoming?

My journey to practise simplicity was made possible by the solitude created by stepping away from social media for a time. The critical distance allowed me to interrogate my own use in light of these questions: who am I becoming in my use of this? Am I becoming more or less like Christ? And I discovered an uncomfortable truth: in most cases, scrolling through the visual lives of people I know and those I do not made me either judgmental or envious. Honest confession: either I was glad that my life was not like theirs or I became acutely aware of where my life fell short from the vision of the good life that had captured my imagination. As a result, I could not see that my life was a gift and, thus, I was unable to receive it wholeheartedly or gratefully. Rather, I only saw what I lacked. From experience, I can tell you that when this is the lens through which we see the world, judgment and envy lead to disconnection from others, with isolation and loneliness following not far behind. Seeking the kingdom of God, marked by gratitude for the good gifts of God, had fallen to the wayside and I was tempted to chase the illusion of the life I felt I should (or deserved to) have.

The other sharp realization I had was how my use of social media had created a duplicity within me. While my online life was me, it was a curated version of me, and this spilled into my analogue life. As I went about my day, I was no longer paying attention to the moment but, instead, how I could update my status to capture the essence of the moment in a witty and clever way. I started to see the world as possible photos to post, imagining how I would crop the world to squares and apply filters to make it look better than real life. I found myself resonating with Turkle's observation: 'In theory, you know the difference between yourself and your Facebook self. But lines blur and it can be hard to keep them straight. It's like telling very small lies over time. You forget the truth because it is so close to the lies.'[59] The freedom that comes with the simplicity of being in Christ had been traded for the bondage of duplicity: I wanted to present to whoever would take notice a self and a world that was just a little bit better than reality. Rather than resting in the limitation of my creatureliness, I had stepped into the role of creator, making a false world that took me further away from who I truly was.

I wanted to present a self and a world that was just a little bit better than reality

Fasting from social media gave the Spirit the space to work in my life, recalibrating my sense of identity and rooting it once again in God. As I have stepped back into this sphere, to practise simplicity has required that I limit the extent to which social media forms my imagination, meaning my use is severely curtailed, with periods of no activity. I do not always get this right and, just as easily as anyone else, I can get drawn into the vision of life that social media curates. However, while this is the case, I have found that I am now quicker in identifying when I have believed the deception, because I now know the freedom and beauty of seeking first God's kingdom. I still kick against my limitations, but I am learning that who I truly am is found within them. From this place, I am learning to stop—our final discipline.

Questions for Reflection

- What visions of the good life have captured your imagination? Where have these visions become distractions from seeking first God's kingdom? What needs to be brought under the control of the Spirit?

- How much of your time are you giving to use of digital technology? Consider keeping a time diary for a week, being honest as you document your activity. What does your time say about what you pay attention to? How is that forming and shaping the way you see the world, yourself, others, and God?
- What marks your online life: simplicity or duplicity? What does it look like to seek integrity in all of your life, digital included?

6 Reimagining the Practice of the Spiritual Disciplines: Sabbath

As we have already considered, the technology of the digital age allows us to (think we can) transcend limitations that were previously non-negotiable, specifically the limitation of time. For example, before the smartphone, work was more easily contained within the working day. While it was always possible to take work home, when we left, we had to leave behind most of the communication devices of work. Now, should we so choose, we can work anywhere and at any time. As the boundaries that demarcated our day have blurred, we now need tools to manage and contain the work, many of which come in the form of apps that further tether us to our digital devices. The capacity and expectation for overwork alongside the driving expectation that we achieve a particular vision of the good life have led us back to an ancient truth: we, as humans, are designed to rest. This has been explored in books that deride the popular exhortation to hustle,[60] teach us to move from a place of hurry to one of presence,[61] and extol the virtues of sleep.[62] The latter was a particular concern for 24/7, an exhibition at London's Somerset House, which explored the 'non-stop nature of modern life.' Their concern? 'With every moment seemingly an opportunity to connect and work, unrelenting pressure to produce and consume, sleep itself monitored and commodified, how we cope is one of the most urgent contemporary issues affecting us all.'[63] The urgency comes because our physical, mental, emotional and relational health is suffering, and in this context, to stop is an act of resistance.

We, as humans, are designed to rest

Giving up Control

For the Christian, the discipline of Sabbath, of stopping, is 'God's gift of repetitive and regular rest…given for our delight and communion with God.'[64] Sabbath stretches back to the creation narrative, grounded in God's rest on the seventh day (Gen 2.2–3). Sabbath rest, '[t]ime for being in the midst of a life of doing,'[65] is part of the fabric of the way the world is and, thus, is fundamental to living well.[66] The challenge to rest is not new. What is also not new is humanity's disobedience to the God-given command. Resting is hard because, by resting, we must face the truth about who we are: we are finite, limited and not in control. Put another way, we are not God. Instead, built into the warp and weft of human living is a daily (sleep) and weekly (Sabbath) reminder that we are creatures, wholly dependent for our very existence on our creator. To practise Sabbath is to worship, to honour the infinite God as we trust that the world is not sustained by our activity. Thus, Sabbath is not simply a discipline but a liturgy that orientates us to God in love and worship. James K A Smith reminds us that, '[w]e are what we love, and our love is shaped, primed, and aimed by liturgical practices that take hold of our gut and aim our heart to certain ends.'[67] When we practise Sabbath, when we go through the motions of resting for 24 hours and worshipping the one we love, even if we do not want to, the action of our body begins to reform our hearts. By stopping, we receive God's good gift to his creatures, time for rest, time for renewal and time for recreation. By stopping in our work, our body leads our heart in an act of trust. We physically demonstrate our rejection of the lie that God is bound by our time economy and step into the truth that God is the all-powerful creator of the world.

By stopping, we receive God's good gift to his creatures

The call to extend Sabbath to our use of digital technology is persistent in contemporary writing.[68] In some instances, even the language is the same, such as doctors advocating a 'screen-free Sabbath.'[69] Those writing outside of the Christian tradition are identifying, although not consciously, that the way God designed us to live in the world is necessary for our flourishing. We need sacred, set aside, space and time in order to be present to God, to each other, and to ourselves. Sabbath in a digital age requires that we carve particular-to-our-age patterns of living that include resting from the digital.

This starts with daily practice. In addition to being intentional about where we put our phones when we sleep, it also means turning off our screens an hour before bed so that we align with how God designed our bodies to wind down.[70] While an inconvenient truth, contrary to burning the candle at both ends, to sleep is to receive our limitation with gratitude. Extending daily rest to weekly rest then follows. Longer times of withdrawal allow us to put a literal plug in the incessant flow of information and possibility available to us. The quantity of information we receive is now far beyond what we can process in a meaningful or discerning way. By stopping the flow, we are gifted with the opportunity to take a step back and gain perspective, while being granted space to listen for the voice of God.

Sabbath in Practice: Removing the Barrier to True Connection

Practising Sabbath has never been easy for me. I grew up in a Christian tradition that saw Sabbath as one of the practices we were set free from with the coming of Christ. Thus, to keep Sabbath was seen as legalistic, and rather than examine the practice with nuance, it was discarded. In its place came the conditions for overwork and an unsustainable level of productivity. What I learned was that you can only go against the design of God for so long; in his great mercy, God brought me to a place of rest, necessitated by circumstances outside of my control. Through this, I had to receive the gift of stopping, which was life-transforming. A day of rest is now a regular part of my routine. However, the expression of Sabbath did not extend to digital technology. I rested from work, yes, but I was still tethered to my phone and the worlds to which it connected me. As I wrestled with the content of this booklet, I felt the nudge of the Spirit once again.

While 24 hours of a screen-free Sabbath seems unrealistic (but this might change), the first step has been to leave my phone at home when I go to church on Sunday. Without fail, every Sunday involves an internal argument as to why I might need my phone that day. However, as I close the front door, I feel a palpable sense of freedom. What has been most surprising is how this practice has impacted my experience at church. Without my phone, I have noticed that my mind and heart are able to prepare and be present to the worship of God, something that I expected to be the case. However, what surprised me was the impact on relationship with others. When I enter church without my phone, I enter without a barrier to interaction with others. I not only say hello more readily but also open myself up to be welcomed into the community. Because I am not distracted, there is no low-level annoyance when I am interrupted by others. I do not have to battle with paying attention because there is no competition. Further, when there is a lull in the service or a moment of discomfort or boredom, there is no phone to tempt me with a quick glance that, truth be told, is never quick. Instead, I have had to persist in the moment and refocus on what God is doing in and around me.

Without my phone, my mind and heart are able to prepare and be present to the worship of God

For me, this practice of Sabbath required physical distance between myself and my phone. While I can choose not to use my phone when I have it with me, the physical distance means it is not an option. Thus, it is not a battle that I have to give energy to fighting. My mind and spirit can rest with my body. Further, conversely to my fears of missing out, what I have realized is that the presence of my phone had been the means of missing out. Without even realizing it, not only had I been missing out on the depth and richness of real community, but also I had closed myself off to the transforming work of the Spirit by allowing my phone to distract me from God's presence.

Questions for Reflection

- How do you feel when you think about adopting the practice of Sabbath? Take some time to reflect on why you feel the way you do. What might lie behind those feelings?
- How will you ensure your daily and weekly practices allow you to rest? What do you need to stop? What do you need to start?
- Sabbath is an individual as well as corporate act. What does a 'screen-free' Sabbath look like for you? For your household and wider community? For your church? Who do you need to invite into the practice? What does accountability look like for you?

Ending

7

This is my story; yours will be different, thus changing the particularities of the practice. However, wherever you are, we begin to practice faithfulness by taking notice of the story we are telling ourselves, the narrative that has captured our imagination and thus formed our beliefs and actions.[71] What does your current use of digital technology say about what you desire, love and worship? From here, what does it mean for you to be conformed to the image of Christ in a digital age? Known by the church and alluded to in contemporary writing, the spiritual practices of the Christian faith align us with the rhythms that God built into his creation. Through them, we come to understand who we truly are—finite and loved creatures—because we come to know who God is. As we practise faithfulness in a digital age, we must be 'wise as serpents and innocent as doves' (Matt 10.16), aware that there is a battle for our souls, our attention and our love. And it is the disciplines that we must reimagine, recovering their service to the Spirit for our formation into the likeness of Christ.

What does it mean for you to be conformed to the image of Christ in a digital age?

Notes

1 S Schumacher, 'The Renewal of your Mind—Reconnecting in the Digital Age: Social Media and Community,' *htb Focus,* Lecture, 26 July 2016.

2 N Carr, *The Shallows: What the Internet is Doing to Our Brains* (New York: W W Norton and Company, 2011).

3 An early example of this is E Brooks and P Nicholas, *Virtually Human: Flourishing in a Digital World* (Nottingham: InterVarsity Press, 2015).

4 For recent Christian writing on this, see J Bethke, *To Hell with the Hustle* (Nashville, TN: Nelson Books, 2019); J M Comer, *The Ruthless Elimination of Hurry: How to Stay Emotionally Healthy and Spiritually Alive in the Chaos of the Modern World* (London: Hodder and Stoughton, 2019); J W Earley, *The Common Rule: Habits of Purpose for an Age of Distraction* (Downers Grove, IL: InterVarsity Press, 2019).

5 J D Hunter, *To Change the World: The Irony, Tragedy, and Possibility of Christianity in the Late Modern World* (Oxford University Press, 2010) p 211.

6 For more, see A Spadaro, *Cybertheology: Thinking Christianity in the Era of the Internet*, Maria Way (trans) (New York: Fordham University Press, 2014).

7 For more, including the impact of AI and robots on social interaction, see S Turkle, *Alone Together: Why We Expect More from Technology and Less from Each* Other (New York: Basic Books, 2011).

8 C Newport, *Digital Minimalism: On Living Better with Less Technology* (London: Penguin Business, 2019).

9 S Turkle, *Reclaiming Conversation: The Power of Talk in a Digital Age* (New York: Penguin, 2015).

10 S Pinker, *The Village Effect: How Face-to-Face Contact Can Make Us Healthier and Happier* (Toronto: Vintage Canada, 2015).

11 A Alter, *Irresistible: The Rise of Addictive Technology and the Business of Keeping us Hooked* (New York: Penguin, 2017).

12 Newport, *op cit,* pp 59-81.

13 Turkle, *op cit,* pp 59-78.

14 Alter, *op cit,* pp 365-406.

15 R Foster, *Celebration of Discipline: The Path to Spiritual Growth*, twentieth anniversary edition (New York: HarperCollins, 1998) p 2.

16 *ibid*, p 1.

17 *ibid*, p 7.

18 A Ahlberg Calhoun, *Spiritual Disciplines Handbook: Practices that Transform Us* (Downers Grove, IL: InterVarsity Press, 2005) p 18.

19 Foster, *op cit,* pp 9-11.

20 For more on this distinction, see J K A Smith, *Desiring the Kingdom: Worship, Worldview, and Cultural Formation* (Grand Rapids, MI: Baker Academic, 2009) pp 188–189.

21 R Bauckham, *God and the Crisis of Freedom: Biblical and Contemporary Perspectives* (Louisville, TN: Westminster John Knox Press, 2002) p 155.

22 See Bethke, *op cit* and Comer, *op cit*.

23 S Hauerwas, 'The Politics of Gentleness' in S Hauerwas, J Vanier and J Swinton (eds), *Living Gently in a Violent World: The Prophetic Witness of Weakness* (Downers Grove, IL: InterVarsity Press, 2008) p 70.

24 Comer, *op cit,* p 95.

25 Newport, *op cit,* p 103.

26 *ibid*, p 109.

27 Turkle, *op cit,* p 46.

28 *ibid*, p 47.

29 Ahlberg Calhoun, *op cit*, p 111.

30 Newport, *op cit,* p 103.

31 Ahlberg Calhoun, *op cit*, p 111.

32 Foster, *Celebration of Discipline, op cit*, p 97.

33 *ibid*, p 96.

34 *ibid.*

35 *ibid*, p 10.

36 Turkle, *op cit,* p 23.

37 Foster, *Celebration of Discipline, op cit,* pp 105–106.

38 Newport, *op cit,* pp 100–101.

39 Alter, *op cit,* p 25.

40 Newport, *op cit*, pp 59–81.

41 R Foster, *Freedom of Simplicity* (London: SPCK, 1981) pp 12–13.

42 M Kondo, *The Life-Changing Magic of Tidying Up: The Japanese Art of Decluttering and Organizing*, English version (Berkeley: Ten Speed Press, 2014); *Tidying Up with Marie Kondo*, directed by Jade Sandberg Wallis, written by Marie Kondo, *Netflix*, 2019.

43 Ahlberg Calhoun, *op cit,* p 74.

44 For more, see Smith, *op cit.*

45 *ibid*, pp 39–73.

46 Alter, *op cit,* p 19.

47 *ibid*, pp 10–14.

48 Newport, *op cit,* p 135.

49 Pinker, *op cit*, pp 9–13.

50 Newport, *op cit,* p 152.

51 Alter, *op cit,* pp 152–155.

52 *ibid*, p 38.

53 Foster, *Celebration of Discipline, op cit,* p 91.

54 Alter, *op cit,* p 382.

55 Alter, *op cit,* p 87.

56 I first came across the idea in E Brooks and P Nicholas, *op cit,* p 67.

57 Such as Psalm 1, 5, 65 and 92.

58 Foster, *Celebration of Discipline, op cit,* p 91.

59 Turkle, *op cit*, p 84.

60 Bethke, *op cit.*

61 Comer, *op cit.*

62 M Walker, *Why We Sleep: The New Science of Sleep and Dreams* (New York: Scribner, 2017).

63 '24/7: A Wake-up Call for our Non-Stop World,' Exhibition, Somerset House, accessed 12 March 2020, https://www.somersethouse.org.uk/whats-on/247

64 Ahlberg Calhoun, *op cit,* p 40.

65 *ibid.*

66 For more, see M Scarlata, *Sabbath Rest: The Beauty of God's Rhythm for a Digital Age* (London: SCM Press, 2019).

67 Smith, *op cit,* p 40.

68 Newport, *op cit,* p 166.

69 Dr R Chatterjee, *The 4 Pillar Plan: How to Relax, Eat, Move, Sleep your Way to a Longer, Healthier Life* (London: Penguin Random House, 2018) pp 36–43.

70 *ibid,* p 216.

71 For more about the relationship between desire and practice, see Smith, *op cit.*